Marvellous Magic

by
Clare Oliver

The Magic Castle
The Magic Castle is a place where magicians meet and perform their own brand of marvellous magic.

MAGIC QUIZ

Who performed 225 different magic tricks in two minutes?
a) Speedy Gonzales
b) Way Fasto
c) Dr Eldoonie

Who first pulled a rabbit out of a hat?
a) John Henry Anderson
b) the Great Myxomatosis
c) Bugsy Lapin

Who was famous for 'vanishing' a caged canary?
a) the Human Stomach
b) Oscar Wilde
c) Carl Hertz

(answers on page 32)

DOVE TALE

Producing white doves is another of the classic feats in the conjurer's repertoire. But the Great Tomsoni performed this trick with a hilarious twist. His doves always covered his dinner jacket with droppings!

A QUACKING GOOD SHOW

One of Alexander Hermann's favourite tricks was to pull a live duck out of a coconut shell. Legend has it that he also once threw a sultan's watch into the sea. The sultan was furious – until Hermann caught a fish, sliced it open, and revealed the watch safe and sound inside.

MONUMENTAL MAGIC

In 1983, an American magician made one of the world's most famous monuments disappear. Before a crowd of spectators, and filmed from above by a helicopter, David Copperfield screened off the Statue of Liberty. When the screen was lowered, the statue had vanished into thin air! It was the biggest outdoor illusion ever seen. Copperfield has also 'disappeared' a seven-tonne Lear jet and an Orient Express train carriage! Doing such tricks have made him an international celebrity and millionaire.

NOW YOU SEE IT... NOW YOU DON'T

Think of a magician, and chances are you'll imagine a white rabbit being pulled from a top hat. And though very few performers work with rabbits these days, they are all masters of illusion, able to make things vanish or to produce the most amazing objects as if from nowhere.

White dove

WHITE RABBITS!

The so-called Wizard of the North, John Henry Anderson, christened his rabbit-out-of-a-hat trick *The Great Chapeau Feat*. Queen Victoria loved Anderson's show so much that she gave the Scottish sorcerer a huge diamond ring!

The Great Chapeau Feat

EGG-CITING TRICKERY

In the 1860s, top American magician Antonio Blitz wowed Abraham Lincoln by pulling a whole egg out of the president's mouth!

CUPS, BALLS & RINGS

Every magician has a favourite trick, but some, such as the *Cups and Balls* and the *Chinese Linking Rings*, are classic illusions that have astounded audiences for centuries.

MADE IN CHINA

The Chinese Linking Rings

The *Chinese Linking Rings* trick uses up to eight solid metal rings. With just this simple set – and some clever sleight of hand – the magician separates and interlinks the rings. An expert magician can even throw separate rings into the air and make them fall back into his hands linked together in a chain!

IN THEIR CUPS

In different countries, magicians used whatever materials came to hand as props for *Cups and Balls*. Japanese conjurers used silken cups, and the Turks used balls of cork. Cork, usually wrapped up in some sort of fabric, remains a favourite with modern magicians.

TRICK CHICK

Egyptian conjurers, known as *galli galli*, had their own version of the *Cups and Balls* – the *Cups and Chicks*! They moved around live chicks under their cups.

ROMAN REMAINS

Ancient Roman conjurers used a vinegar jar, which they called *acetabulum*, for their *Cups and Balls* trick. It must have been their favourite trick because Roman magicians were called *acetabularii*.

Performing the Cups and Balls trick

MAGIC QUIZ

Which Roman writer described the *Cups and Balls* trick?

a) Pope Innocent II
b) Roman Polanski
c) Seneca the Younger

Which artist included the *Cups and Balls* trick in a painting?

a) Pablo Picasso
b) Hieronymus Bosch
c) Michelangelo

What was another name for the *Cups and Balls* trick?

a) Thimble-rig
b) Mugs and Balls
c) Cups and Thimbles

(answers on page 32)

CUPS & BALLS

No one knows who first performed *Cups and Balls*, but the ancient Greek Alciphron of Athens wrote about it nearly 1,800 years ago. The conjurer usually starts with three balls under three cups. Then the balls move, appear, and disappear, and even seem to pass through the tops of the cups. Often for the finale, the balls are transformed beneath the cups into one larger, surprising object, such as an orange or a lemon!

5

HOLY POWERS

Hindu holy men (*sadhus*) believe that willpower is a gift of God. Their strong self-discipline enables them to perform amazing feats. They visit fairs, called *melas*, where they walk across scorching-hot coals or recline on a bed of spiky nails. Such tricks are extremely dangerous so don't even think about trying them yourself!

Fire walking

MAGIC QUIZ

What was Sheshal's nickname?

a) the Madras Floater
b) the Air Brahmin
c) the Human Balloon

What is it called when an object is moved by the power of the mind?

a) brainstorming
b) psychokinesis
c) tyrannous

Who levitated himself while riding a bicycle?

a) Henry Roltair
b) Shabu Shabu
c) Walter Raleigh

(answers on page 32)

HIGH-FLIER

Human beings can't fly – or can they? One of the highlights of David Copperfield's stage show is when he propels himself and a member of the audience through the air, flying as if by magic!

CUTLERY MAGIC

The legendary Uri Geller is famous for his cutlery-bending tricks. He seems to reshape metal objects with the sheer power of his will. He even decorated his custom-built Cadillac with 5,000 of his bent forks, knives and spoons.

MIND OVER MATTER

A flourish of a magic wand or saying 'Abracadabra' may seem impressive, but the spookiest magic seems to happen simply because a magician wills it. People can even be made to levitate (hover in mid-air) with nothing to hold them up...

Levitating

UP IN THE AIR

In the 1820s, a man called Sheshal performed levitation for the high society of Madras in India. He sat in mid-air for an hour at a time and made a lot of money from his shows. In 1867, British magician John Nevil Maskelyne brought this magic trick to the West when he caused his wife to levitate at Crystal Palace in London. Maskelyne's son carried on the tradition and passed a hoop over his floating assistant to prove there were no strings attached.

MAGIC MONK

St Joseph of Copertino was always levitating. He once dropped his sandals mid-service onto the heads of a church congregation!

DATE WITH DEATH

Not even an expert escapologist can escape death. Spookily, Harry Houdini predicted he would die at Hallowe'en. And he did. Having heard that Houdini's stomach could withstand the hardest blow, someone punched him before he was ready.

THE GREAT ESCAPE

Some entertainers can wriggle out of the trickiest spots. Escapologists get out of locked bank vaults or padlocked crates – even when they have been shackled or tied up in ropes or chains.

TENKO'S TANK

Japanese illusionist Princess Tenko is one of the few female escapologists. During her glamorous act, she performs a nail-biting escape from a locked metal cage – in a tank full of water!

Princess Tenko

PRIDE IN THE JOB

British escapologist Alan Alan once escaped after being tied by his feet from a burning rope while wearing a straitjacket! Not scary enough for you? Well, waiting beneath him was a pride of very hungry lions! Luckily, Alan managed to escape in just a few seconds.

MOVIE MAGIC

The greatest escapologist of all time was Harry Houdini. For his *Chinese Water Torture* act he was handcuffed and chained up inside a water-filled metal box. Assistants stood by to break open the box if the stunt went wrong but the Amazing Houdini always escaped in time. He also starred in some early Hollywood films which, of course, always featured a daringly difficult escape!

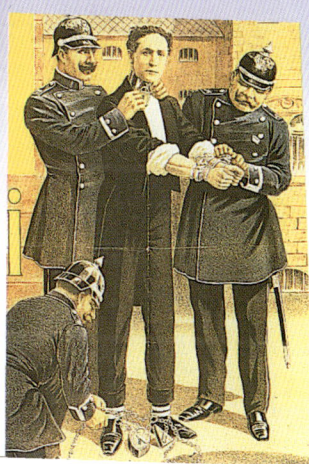

Houdini being handcuffed before an escape

WATER WORLD

Australian escapologist Les Levante used to be tied up and locked into a box on a ship, then thrown overboard! But the skilful Levante never drowned. He always slipped through the ropes, broke through the box, and swam safely up to the surface. Wat-er relief!

MAGIC QUIZ

From which famous prison did David Copperfield escape in 1987?
a) Alcatraz
b) Wormwood Scrubs
c) the Bastille

What is a straitjacket?
a) a coat with sleeves that are long enough to restrain a violent person
b) a coat from the Straits of Gibraltar
c) a coat with no buttons or decoration

What was Houdini's stinkiest escape?
a) from inside a dead whale
b) from inside a sewer
c) from a gasworks

(answers on page 32)

MAGIC QUIZ

Who were the two film comedians who performed the *Indian Rope Trick* (very badly)?

a) Ren and Stimpy
b) Pencil and String
c) Laurel and Hardy

Which Indian magician loved the *Indian Rope Trick*?

a) Ganga
b) Gandhi
c) Sorcar

When did Ibn Battutah describe the *Rope Trick*?

a) 1855
b) 1555
c) 1355

(answers on page 32)

TRICKED TO BITS

The Muslim traveller Ibn Battutah was the first to write about the *Indian Rope Trick*. In China – not India! – he saw an illusionist throw a ball into the air with long leather thongs attached to it. A young boy climbed up the thongs but didn't come back down when called. So, wielding an enormous knife, the conjurer followed. To the horror of his audience, he then tossed down pieces of the boy before sliding back down the thong covered in blood. But it was all a trick and after a few minutes he made the boy reappear, alive and well!

ROPE HOPE

In the *Indian Rope Trick*, the magician first throws a rope into the air. As if by magic, it stays there! Then a child or assistant climbs up the rope and out of sight. The Magic Circle (see page 31) have offered a big reward to any magician who'll perform the trick in the open-air, away from stage curtains. Strangely, no one has yet taken up the challenge!

10

SLIPPERY SORCERY

Some magicians are so sure of their special powers they happily risk their lives with poisonous snakes. How do snake charmers manage to control the coolest customers of the reptile world? And how do other magicians get a lifeless length of rope to behave like a snake?

Snake charmer

CHARMING!

The first-ever International Snake Charmers Competition was held in Malaysia in 1997. About 40 charmers competed for the top prize of $2,000 (about £1,250). Stunts included holding the head of a poisonous snake in the mouth. Some illusionists – very wisely – prefer to do their own version of snake charming, using a piece of rope!

ON A ROLL!

Magician Mike Caveney doesn't use a snake or a rope for his *Indian Rope Trick*. He uses a roll of loo paper!

KING COBRA

One of the world's most venomous snakes, the cobra is a favourite with snake charmers. As the charmer plays his flute or pipe, the snake seems to sway rhythmically. Maybe it picks up on the vibrations of the music, or perhaps it is copying the movement of its musical master. Whatever the reason, the reptile slowly rears up. And although one in ten cobra bites prove fatal, the snake isn't a speedy mover, so the charmer is rarely hurt.

Cobra

MAGIC QUIZ

Which of these is a fictional school of magic?
a) Hogwarts
b) Pigmoles
c) Sowspots

Which is the world's oldest magic shop?
a) Tannen's, New York
b) Flourish and Blotts, London
c) Père Roujol's, Paris

Which of these is not a famous magic shop?
a) Davenports
b) Bloomingdales
c) Martinka's

(answers on page 32)

ACE ACCESSORIES

While silk handkerchiefs, coins, or a deck of cards are essential for certain tricks, other accessories are only needed to distract people's attention while you perform a nifty switch. These could include a magic wand, tall top hat, elegant white gloves, or even a flowing cape. But many modern magicians choose their own individual stage style. German illusionists Siegfried and Roy wear glitzy outfits straight out of the 70s, while Yuka Simada is known for her traditional Japanese kimono and elegant paper fans.

A cape or top hat helps you look the part

An essential tool for any young magician – the magic wand

Show the audience how you escape with your hands tied in chains, like Houdini

Cards can be used for many amazing tricks

THE MAGICIAN'S APPRENTICE

No real-life school timetable has 'conjuring' or 'sleight of hand' on it - so just how do you learn to be a magician?

PRACTICE MAKES PERFECT

Young magicians need to practise. Most invest in a simple box of magic props. They also need instruction – a book of step-by-step tricks to perform, or a video with close-ups of the magician's art. Even so, mastering the most basic tricks can seem to take forever.

HEROES AND HOPE

As with anything, the first step to becoming a magician is really wanting to be one. Most successful magicians remember as a child seeing an amazing trick and knowing in that instant that they would do anything to be able to perform magic.

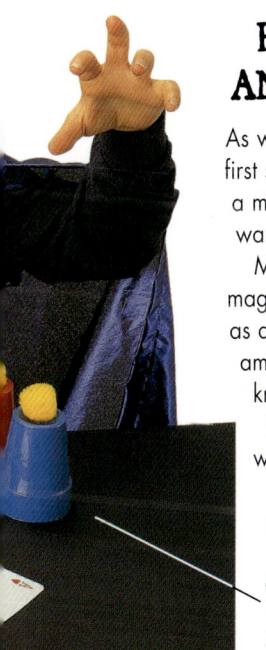

Cups and Balls

TAKING THE MICKEY

One of the most famous learner magicians was a mouse – Mickey Mouse! The film *Fantasia* was one of Disney's most magical films!

Fortune-teller

MAGIC QUIZ

Where did ancient Greeks go to find their fortune?
a) Allied Oracles of Sparta and Athens
b) Oracle at Corfu
c) Oracle at Delphi

Where are the most runestones?
a) Norway
b) Sweden
c) Denmark

What is another word for foretelling the future?
a) divination
b) futuramavision
c) swine-swindling

(answers on page 32)

PROPER BUSINESS

Fortune-tellers use all manner of props. The classic crystal ball is said to contain a milky mist that clears to reveal a vision. Tarot cards have been around for nearly 600 years. Much older are the hexagrams of the Chinese *I-Ching* (*Book of Changes*), which are used to predict the outcome of possible actions.

RUNE MAGIC

The Vikings and some Germanic peoples used mysterious symbols called runes to decorate their armour, jewellery and other artefacts. They also inscribed runic symbols on stones. On the rune stone on Frösön Island in Lake Storsjön, Sweden, runes form the shape of a serpent around its edge. Legend has it that the magical powers of the runes bind a monster in the lake. The day someone manages to decipher the runes, the monster will escape!

POT LUCK

Make a pot of tea using tea leaves and pour a cupful without using a strainer. As you drink, think of a question. Swirl the leftover dregs onto a saucer. The shape the leaves make is the answer to your question. (Chances are you'll interpret them to mean whatever you want them to!)

WHAT THE FUTURE HOLDS

If you ever read your horoscope, surprisingly it may seem to come true. Cynics aren't surprised, though. They claim horoscopes are so vague they could relate to almost any event!

IN YOUR PALM

Palmists 'read' hands to see a person's character or to predict such things as how long they will live or whether they'll meet their perfect partner!

Life Line – *represents your spirit and how much you put into your life*
Head Line – *represents the kind of mind you have*
Heart Line – *represents your feelings and how well you get on with people*
Fate Line – *represents how successful or lucky you'll be*
Marriage Lines – *represents your closest special relationships*
Health Line – *represents how healthy – or sickly! – you'll be*

HALLO, TAROT

The tarot is read to work out a subject's character and to make a prediction. A specific number of cards are shuffled and dealt face-down in certain shapes. The cards are then interpreted. *The Magician* card may indicate the person has strong willpower or is skilful.

Stonehenge

STANDING STONES

One of the amazing feats credited to Merlin is the building of Stonehenge, the prehistoric stone circle on Salisbury Plain, Wiltshire. No one can explain how or why the massive stones – some weighing as much as 25 tonnes – were put there. Did the stones have some magical significance?

In 1963, one wacky American astronomer, Gerald Hawkins, said that the stones were used as a primitive computer for predicting eclipses!

EVIL MAGIC

According to legend, Merlin's arch enemy was the fairy queen, Morgan le Fay. Merlin brought Arthur up to protect him from her evil power, but he was unable to do the same for Arthur's nephew, Mordred. Morgan taught Mordred all the magic she knew and Arthur met his death at Mordred's hand.

MAGIC QUIZ

When did people start building Stonehenge?

a) after a big breakfast
b) once they'd found the stones
c) 3100 BC

Who or what was the Holy Grail?

a) the cup used by Christ at the Last Supper
b) a precious stone that had fallen from heaven
c) the cup used to catch Christ's blood as he hung on the cross

What beast did Uther Pendragon wear on his coat of arms?

a) dragon
b) phoenix
c) unicorn

(answers on page 32)

TREE TRAP

The Lady in the Lake persuaded Merlin to teach her magic – then used what she'd learnt to imprison him forever inside an old oak tree.

16

MARVELLOUS MERLIN

Wizard and counsellor to King Arthur, Merlin is the most famous wizard of all time. He may or may not have existed, but his legend lives on in movies such as *Excalibur*.

THE ROUND TABLE

Merlin's protégé Arthur set up the Knights of the Round Table, a brotherhood of brave, pure-hearted knights that included Galahad, Lancelot and Gawain. These young men went off on quests, such as finding the Holy Grail. Merlin is said to have built the Round Table for Arthur's father, Uther Pendragon. Later, it came into the hands of King Leodegran of Carmelide. When Arthur married Leodegran's daughter, Guinevere, the table was given to Arthur as a wedding present.

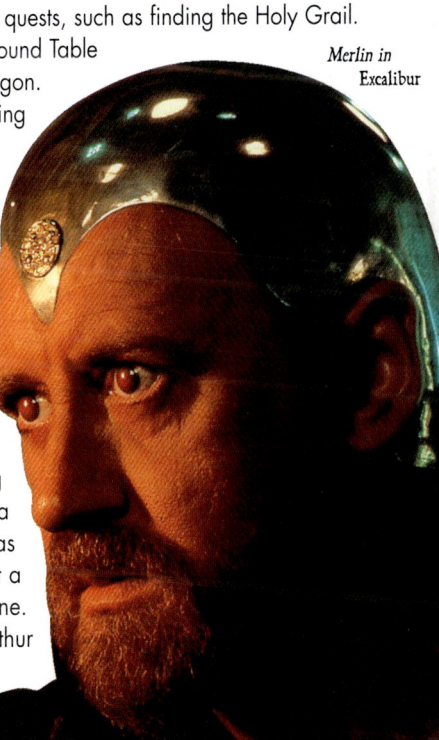

Merlin in Excalibur

SPECIAL SWORD

Merlin trained the young Arthur and helped him to become King of the Britons. Merlin devised a magical test to prove Arthur was true heir to the throne. He set a sword called Excalibur into a stone. Many tried but only young Arthur was able to pull it out.

CUTTING-EDGE MAGIC

When an illusionist saws his assistant in half, it's hard to believe your eyes! One minute she's all in one piece, the next, she's literally gone to pieces! Ambulances stand by in case anything goes wrong. It never does because the trick can only be performed with special 'magic' equipment.

I SAW SORCAR...

Champion of *Sawing a Woman in Half* was the great Indian magician Pratul Chandra Sorcar. With his bejewelled turban he seemed very exotic to Western audiences of the 1950s. But Sorcar was less traditional when he performed the trick. To add scary suspense, he used a motorised buzzsaw and didn't bother to hide his assistant in a box!

OOPS!

Some magicians put their assistants back together the wrong way – on purpose! The joke is part of the illusion.

ONE SMALL CUT FOR WOMANKIND

Hilarious illusionist Paula Paul has her own version of *Sawing a Woman in Half*. She calls her trick *Sawing a Man in Half*!

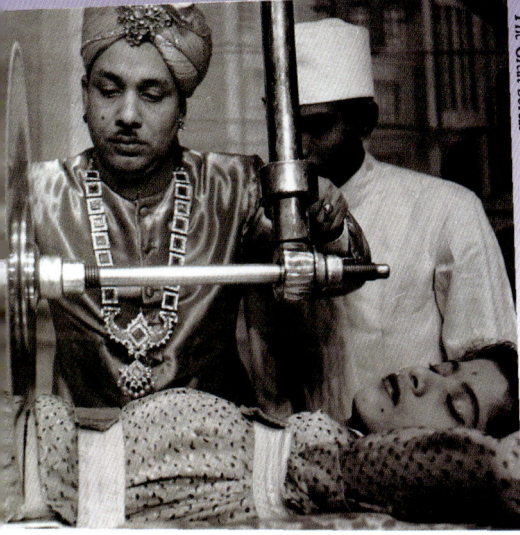

The Great Sorcar

CUT-OUT

The Great Sorcar was making his first appearance on British television when the broadcast suddenly cut out in mid-act! The phone lines jammed as thousands of viewers phoned in to find out if his assistant, Dipty Dey, was OK. She was!

MAGIC QUIZ

What does David Copperfield use to cut people in half?
a) laser
b) penknife
c) cheese knife

Which illusionists turn the blade on themselves?
a) sword swallowers
b) politicians
c) home economics teachers

Who first 'sawed a woman in half'?
a) P.T. Selbit
b) Sorcar
c) Robert Harbin

(answers on page 32)

Look, no body!

ZIG-ZAG GIRL

South African magician Robert Harbin introduced a new version of the trick in 1965. He used the traditional box but cut holes in it so that the audience never lost sight of his assistant's body. He sliced the box into three and slid the middle section to one side, to create the Zig-Zag Girl. Her face, belly button and toes could be seen in three different places!

MAGIC QUIZ

Which of these actors hangs out with David Blaine?

a) Tobey Maguire
b) Lukas Haas
c) Leonardo DiCaprio

What is passing around a hat for money called?

a) the throw
b) the collection
c) the finale

Who wrote a book about being a street magician?

a) Ace Starry
b) Ronald Reagan
c) Harry Houdini

(answers on page 32)

CLEVER CHATTER

No amount of planning will keep the attention of an audience if the show is no good. Performances are kept short so people don't rush off, but it's fast and clever patter as well as fantastic tricks that keep them hooked – and make them happy to part with their cash!

PAVEMENT PERFORMANCE

Successful street entertainers have all sorts of attention-grabbing tricks up their sleeves. They never choose a spot where the Sun is behind them. People would be busy screwing up their eyes and would not be able to see the show! The entertainers try to find places where there's a natural stage, such as on a flight of steps or in a public square. Some even set up a play clock to advertise the time of their next show. If people know one is about to start, they may stick around to see it.

SECRETS UNVEILED!

It's against the magicians' code to reveal secrets to lay people, but in recent years there have been TV shows that do just that. Street Magic hasn't escaped. In November 1999, a mysterious Masked Magician exposed more than 24 tricks to American television viewers. He was masked to protect his identity – other magicians might have decided to teach him a lesson.

David Blaine. Now you see him..

OUT ON THE STREET

Sleight-of-hand tricks have been performed for passers-by on the street for centuries. Today, the coolest young entertainers on the block are championing the art of Street Magic.

BURIED ALIVE!

Leader of the pack is David Blaine, a handsome American with smooth-talking 'patter'. One of his most impressive illusions was to bury himself alive in front of Trump Towers in New York. He was lowered into the ground in a clear coffin. Then, before the stunned spectators' very eyes, he vanished into thin air! Blaine remained underground for a week and attracted thousands of spectators. The stunt was televised and his show, *David Blaine: Street Magic*, created even more devoted fans.

ROCK ON

Blaine has a cool story of what turned him on to magic. As a boy he had a pet rock, then one day a man on the underground turned his rock into a crystal. Wow!

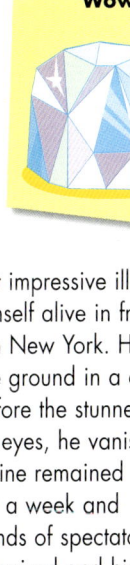

Now you don't!

MAGIC QUIZ

In which Shakespeare play does a fairy queen feature?
a) *Macbeth*
b) *A Midsummer Night's Dream*
c) *Romeo and Juliet*

What must you never do in Fairyland if you want to be able to go home?
a) eat or drink
b) sing
c) poke fun at the fairies

Which famous fairy appears in *Peter Pan*?
a) Stinkerbell
b) Tinkerbell
c) Winkandtell

(answers on page 32)

FAIRY TALES

Storybook fairies haven't always been 5 cm tall with fluttering wings. In medieval tales, fairies could be as big as human beings and even kidnapped small children. But their cruel image was banished forever by Victorian storytellers and illustrators such as Cicely Mary Barker, with her stunning *Flower Fairies of the Garden*.

Dandelion Fairy

ANIMAL MAGIC

There are many myths that involve animals. The Norse goddess Freya was said to cross the night sky in a chariot drawn by magical, flying cats. Then there's the ancient Egyptian myth of the phoenix. This was a bird that lived for centuries. When the phoenix became old and tired it set fire to itself. After the flames died down and only ashes remained, a new phoenix emerged to begin life again!

MAGICAL MAKE-BELIEVE

Storybook magic may not amaze like real-life conjuring tricks, but young or old, we all enjoy a magical tale, whether it's about exotic flying carpets in ancient Arabia, or fluttering fairies at the bottom of the garden.

TALES FROM THE ORIENT

A flying carpet

The Arabian Nights' Entertainments is a collection of magical tales supposedly told to a sultan who had a nasty habit of killing his wives. Whenever he came for young Scheherazade, she distracted him by telling another gripping instalment. Her characters are just as popular today and include Sinbad the Sailor, Ali Baba (who foxed the Forty Thieves) and the hero Aladdin. They all make good use of magic, including flying carpets and genies in lamps!

UP, UP & AWAY!

Father Christmas's magical reindeer may have been thought up by the Inuit people. On cold, icy evenings they sometimes ate poisonous mushrooms that made them see visions, such as reindeer flying through the sky!

23

SCIENCE OR MAGIC?

Even today, some scientific discoveries can seem like magic. A few hundred years ago they must have been truly astounding! Conjurers and chemists can both transform things before our very eyes, and some of the earliest chemists thought they could use their new knowledge to do magic...

AMAZING ALCHEMY

Many early scientists devoted their skills to alchemy. Alchemists had two main aims. One was to find out the secret of eternal life and the other was to find a formula for turning common metals, such as copper, into gold. Some alchemists believed in a magical stone called the philosopher's stone, which turned anything it touched into gold. All they had to do was find it!

Dr Dee

FOOL'S GOLD

Alchemists could have learnt a lesson or two from the legendary King Midas. After the god Dionysus granted Midas's wish that all he touched would turn into gold, the greedy king nearly died of starvation!

MOON MAGIC

In 1503, explorer Chistopher Columbus used science to scare the Taino people into giving him food. He told them his God's magic was more powerful than theirs and proved it by making the sky go dark. Crafty Columbus knew all along that an eclipse was due on 29 February.

An eclipse

DR DEE

Dr John Dee, a sixteenth-century mathematician and astrologer, once created some amazing special effects for a stage play. Ever after he was considered to be a master magician. He was certainly very clever and well-read, but also a bit of a con man. Today, scientists would sneer at his theories of 'crystallomancy' and astrology.

CULT OF THE OCCULT

In the 1500s, many clever people believed in a secret key to all existence that could explain the mysteries of religion, magic, science, alchemy and the stars. This was called hermetism and had a strong following for about 200 years. Hermetism is named after Hermes Trismegistus, the ancient Greek name for the Egyptian god Thoth, who invented a magic seal. Even top bods such as Isaac Newton held some hermetic beliefs.

MAGIC QUIZ

How many elements did alchemists think made up the Earth?
a) four: air, water, earth and fire
b) five: air, water, earth, fire and space
c) they weren't sure

Who wrote the play *The Alchemist*?
a) William Shakespeare
b) Ben Jonson
c) Arthur Miller

Where did the Taino Indians live?
a) West Indies
b) Tasmania
c) Tanzania

(answers on page 32)

SINK OR SWIM

Witch-hunters needed a test for witchcraft. One favourite was 'ducking'. The accused person was thrown into the village duckpond. If he or she floated, it was considered cast-iron proof of their magical powers, and guilt. Sinking proved your innocence – but that was small comfort when you drowned!

A FAMILIAR TAIL

Most of the creatures thought to be a witch's shape-shifting familiar were probably just ordinary pets!

The Wicked Witch of the West

BLACK & WHITE

Not all witches are as bad and ugly as the famous Wicked Witch of the West from *The Wizard of Oz*. Some followers of Wicca use their magic powers to do good things, such as healing sick people. Magic that is used to help people is known as white magic. But black magic is followed by wicked witches who want to cause harm.

WITCHES & WIZARDS

Not so long ago people were tried and put to death for being witches. Today, it's OK to admit you're a witch. The witchcraft practised by modern-day witches is known as Wicca. Often, they look as ordinary as your mum and dad!

WITCH HUNTS

From medieval times up to the 1700s, Europe was gripped by witch fever. Thousands of people were hunted down and put on trial for witchcraft. They were accused of possessing magical powers, casting spells on their neighbours, or flying around on broomsticks!

A warty Chinese toad

CREATURE COMFORTS

Traditionally, a black cat or a warty toad would have made a perfect familiar (witch's assistant). A toad could also have doubled up as an ingredient in some of those troubling, bubbling spells!

MAGIC QUIZ

In what does a witch brew magic spells?

a) teapot
b) cauldron
c) beer barrel

What star protects you from witchcraft?

a) five-pointed pentacle
b) seven-pointed star
c) black star

Which US town hosted a terrifying witch trial in 1692?

a) Salem, Oregon
b) Salem, Missouri
c) Salem, Massachusetts

(answers on page 32)

MAGIC OF THE ANCIENTS

Historians of magic often argue over which was the very first trick. It's possible that prehistoric people performed simple tricks to entertain each other in their caves at night. Having magic gods gave leaders power, but the first real evidence of magic comes from the ancient Egyptians.

ANCIENT AMULETS

For the Egyptians, magic and religious beliefs were one and the same. When a person died and was preserved by being wrapped up as a mummy, priests slipped magic charms called amulets in among the bandages. People also carried amulets about with them to ward off evil. The scarab (or dung) beetle was an especially precious charm because it represented the sun god, Re. Another was the Eye of Horus, believed to be able to outstare any evil spirit.

An Egyptian scarab

CHEOPS OFF THEIR HEADS!

The Westcar Papyrus, an ancient Egyptian document, records the amazing tricks of a magician called Dedi. Dedi performed in front of the Pharaoh Cheops. One of his most grisly tricks involved decapitating a goose, a duck and an ox, then putting their heads back on.

The Westcar Papyrus

SNAPPY SORCERY

The Westcar Papyrus also tells of another Egyptian illusionist. Weba-aner could transform a wax model of a crocodile into a full-size real snapping crocodile. Not the sort of trick you'd want to see close-up!

MAGIC QUIZ

Where is the Westcar Papyrus kept today?

a) no one knows
b) Cairo
c) Berlin

When did the Pharaoh Cheops reign?

a) 2575–2465 BC
b) 1075–1465 BC
c) AD 25–65

Where was Pharaoh Cheops buried?

a) Great Pyramids at Giza
b) Valley of the Kings
c) no one knows

(answers on page 32)

DEDI'S MAGIC DIET

Dedi lived to be 110 years old! He reckoned his daily diet of 500 loaves of bread, a shoulder of beef and 100 jugs of beer had something to do with his amazing good health.

MAGIC QUIZ

Which is the world's largest magical society?
a) The Magic Circle
b) International Brotherhood of Magicians
c) Society of American Magicians

What does SYM stand for?
a) Society of Young Magicians
b) Symbolic Brotherhood of Magicians
c) Sulphurous Yellow Mudbaths

What does *MUM* stand for?
a) *Madmen Unmasking Magicians*
b) *Monthly Universal Magic*
c) *Magic, Unity, Might*

(answers on page 32)

UNCLE SAM

The first-ever magic club was the Société Philomagique in Paris. But the Society of American Magicians (SAM) is the oldest one still in existence. It was established on 10 May 1902 in New York. Within a year Ehrich Weiss (Harry Houdini) was a member. Today, there are over 250 different SAM assemblies around the world and the society also has its own newsletter called *MUM*. The club's headquarters is the Magic Castle in Hollywood, which looks rather like a fairytale palace!

Magician Mark Wilson at the Magic Castle

THE GREAT REVEALER

A magical society provides a safe place to discuss magic among people who wish to preserve its mystery so that the tricks will continue to amaze audiences in years to come. Magic clubs have a strict code of silence and they disown any magicians who break it, such as Valentino the Masked Magician. After all, once you know how a trick is done, it loses its magic!

THE MAGIC CIRCLE

It's always good to meet up with friends, swap news and just hang out. And that goes for magicians, too! There are magic societies all over the world, where people pass on the tricks of the trade and learn how to create amazing new illusions. Such societies provide support for magicians, organise conferences on the history of magic and give advice about the latest props and tricks. Most importantly, magic clubs organise training camps for wannabe magicians.

At the Magic Circle

LONDON'S HQ

The Magic Circle, based in London, has been the headquarters for British magicians since 1905. One of its most famous members is Prince Charles. He was accepted as a member after performing a version of the *Cups and Balls*. The club's motto is *Indocilis Privata Loqui*, which means 'not apt to disclose secrets'.

TESTING TIMES

Magicians have to pass really hard exams to reach the top-secret Inner Magic Circle.

31

QUIZ ANSWERS:

Page 2 c, Dr Eldoonie; a, John Henry Anderson; c, Carl Hertz.
Page 5 c, Seneca the Younger; b, Hieronymus Bosch; a, Thimble-rig.
Page 6 b, the Air Brahmin; b, psychokinesis; a, Henry Roltair.
Page 9 a, Alcatraz; a, a coat with sleeves to restrain a violent person; a, from inside a dead whale.
Page 10 c, Laurel and Hardy; c, Sorcar; c, 1355.
Page 12 a, Hogwarts – from the *Harry Potter* books; c, Père Roujol's, Paris; b, Bloomingdales.
Page 14 c, Oracle at Delphi; b, Sweden; a, divination.
Page 16 c, 3100 BC; a,b,c, trick question – all three descriptions have been used in different poems; a, dragon.
Page 19 a, laser; a, sword swallowers; a, P.T. Selbit.
Page 20 a,b,c, trick question – they all do; a, the throw; a, Ace Starry.
Page 22 b, *A Midsummer Night's Dream*; a, eat or drink; b, Tinkerbell.
Page 25 both a and b are true and maybe c is too!; b, Ben Jonson; a, West Indies.
Page 27 b, cauldron; a, five-pointed pentacle; c, Salem, Massachusetts.
Page 29 c, Berlin; a, 2575–2465 BC; a, Great Pyramids at Giza.
Page 30 b, International Brotherhood of Magicians; a, Society of Young Magicians; c, *Magic, Unity, Might*.

Acknowledgements

We would like to thank Phil Clucus, Helen Wire and Elizabeth Wiggans for their assistance.
Cartoons by John Alston.
Copyright © 2000 ticktock *Publishing Ltd.*
First published in Great Britain by ticktock *Publishing Ltd.,*
The Offices in the Square, Hadlow, Tonbridge, Kent TN11 0DD, Great Britain.
All rights reserved.
No part of this publication may be reproduced, stored in a retrieval system, or transmitted in any form or by any means electronic, mechanical, photocopying, recording or otherwise, without prior written permission of the copyright owner.
A CIP catalogue record for this book is available from the British Library.
ISBN 1 86007 177 5

Picture Credits: t = top, b = bottom, c = centre, l = left, r= right, OFC = outside front cover,
OBC = outside back cover, IFC = inside front cover

AKG; 28/29c. Ann Ronan @ Image Select; 9cl, 24/25c. Fortean Picture Library; 6tl, 22/23c. Gamma; IFC & 30c.
Hulton Getty; 6/7c, 18/19t, 31cr. Images Colour Library; 18bl. Museum of Berlin; 29c. Oxford Scientific; 2tr, 25tl.
Rex; 8b, 10/11b, 20/21c, 21bl. Ronald Grant Archive; 17br, 23tr, 26bl. Spectrum Colour Library; 16t.
Tony Stone Images; 3br, 11b, 14tr, 15bl, 27bl.

Picture research by Image Select. Printed in Hong Kong.